BUTTERFLIES
AND
MOTHS

Consulting Editor: Fredric L. Frye, DVM; MS; Fellow,
Royal Society of Medicine

The title of the Spanish edition is *El fascinante mundo de
las mariposas*

All inquiries should be addressed to:
Barron's Educational Series, Inc.
250 Wireless Boulevard
Hauppauge, New York 11788

Library of Congress Catalog Card No. 91-16142

International Standard Book No. 0-8120-4722-2

Library of Congress Cataloging-in-Publication Data

Julivert, Angels.
  [Fascinante mundo de las mariposas. English]
  The fascinating world of butterflies and moths / by Angels
Julivert : illustrations by Francisco Arrendondo.
      p.   cm.
  Translation of: Fascinante mundo de las mariposas.
  Summary: An introduction to the physical characteris-
tics, habits, and natural environment of various kinds of
butterflies and moths.
  ISBN 0-8120-4722-2
  1. Butterflies—Juvenile literature. [1. Butterflies]
I. Arrendondo, Francisco, ill. II. Title.
QL544.2.J8513 1991
595.78'9—dc20
                                                91-16142
                                                   CIP
                                                    AC

Printed in Spain
4   987654

THE FASCINATING WORLD OF...

BUTTERFLIES
AND
MOTHS

by

Angels Julivert

Illustrations by Francisco Arrendondo

BARRON'S

THE ELEGANT BUTTERFLY

Butterflies and moths are insects belonging to the order of **lepidoptera**, which means *scale wings*. Their bodies and wings are covered by many flat scales that provide color.

Another feature exclusive to lepidoptera is the **spiral tubelike proboscis** that can be extended to sip nectar and other liquids that they live on.

Like all insects, their body is divided into three parts: **head, thorax,** and **abdomen.**

In the head are the sense organs, of which sight and smell are the most important. Through their antennae they detect odors. These antennae have very different forms, depending on the species.

Their large, compound eyes, which are made up of many tiny units called **facets**, can detect normally invisible ultraviolet light.

Attached to the thorax are six thin legs and two large pairs of wings.

Lepidoptera need warmth in order to fly. Butterflies obtain this warmth by spreading their wings and exposing them to the sun. Moths, which are night-flying or nocturnal, shake their wings to warm them.

Right: A butterfly extending its wings to warm them. The butterfly shown in the foreground is cleaning its antennae, through which it detects scents.

Below, left: Structure of a butterfly and detail of its head.

Below: Different kinds of antennae:
A. Serrated.
B. Simple.
C. Comb-shaped.

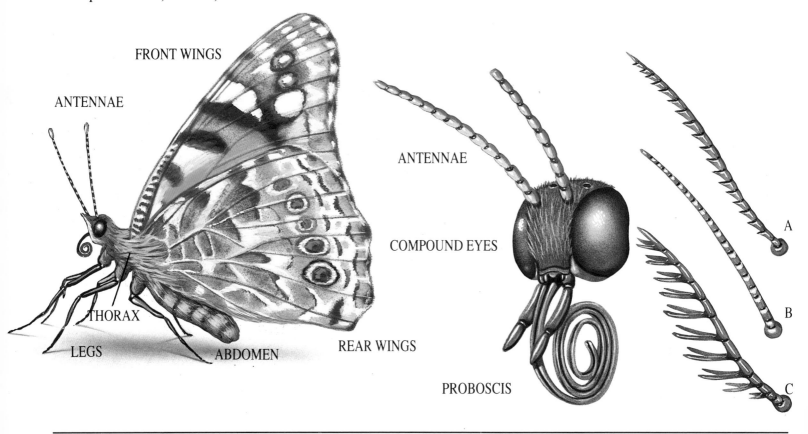

FRONT WINGS

ANTENNAE

THORAX

LEGS

ABDOMEN

REAR WINGS

ANTENNAE

COMPOUND EYES

PROBOSCIS

A

B

C

A MOSAIC OF SHAPES AND COLORS

There are more than 140,000 known species of lepidoptera throughout the world. They can be found in towns, meadows, forests, and woods, as well as in high mountains like the Himalayas.

You would be surprised at the large variety of shapes, sizes, and colors of butterflies and moths. Some of them do not even look like lepidoptera. In fact, there are females of some species who do not have wings.

There are green, blue, and multicolored species, and species with strange designs on their wings. Some of them are very beautiful, but many others are quite plain. Many moths are plain, although some varieties are very attractive.

Not only do the appearances of lepidoptera differ, but also their behavior and habits.

Butterflies usually have lively colors and fold their wings vertically when they are resting.

Unlike their daytime cousins, the nocturnal moths are less beautiful. They have thicker and hairier bodies, and the males have greatly developed antennae.

About 90 percent of the lepidoptera are moths, and many of them are attracted by bright light.

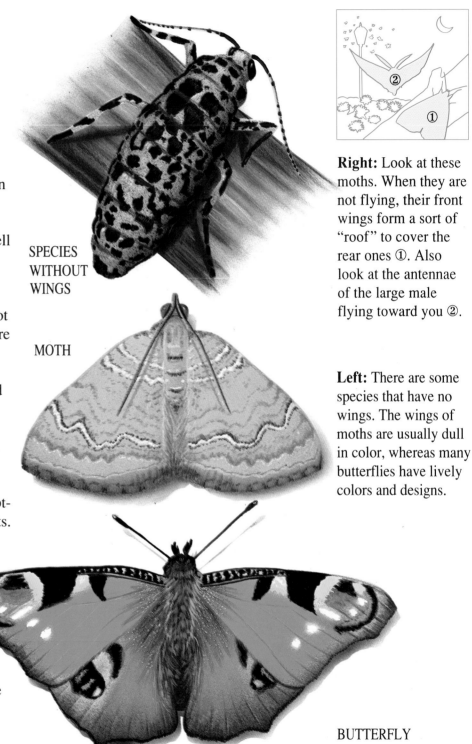

SPECIES WITHOUT WINGS

MOTH

BUTTERFLY

Right: Look at these moths. When they are not flying, their front wings form a sort of "roof" to cover the rear ones ①. Also look at the antennae of the large male flying toward you ②.

Left: There are some species that have no wings. The wings of moths are usually dull in color, whereas many butterflies have lively colors and designs.

LOOKING FOR A PARTNER

Reproduction is essential for the preservation of the species. That is why during certain periods of the year the adult male looks for a partner.

Among the butterflies, the colors and designs on the female's wings attract the males. Some butterflies attract their partners by performing complex flights, and many females emit fragrant substances called **pheromones**.

Moths use scent, not sight, to find their partners. Since they fly at night, colors are quite useless. The female produces pheromones and attracts the male, who, thanks to his sensitive antennae, can detect the smell from quite a distance.

The mating lasts a few minutes. The female lays a large number of eggs––from several hundred to more than a thousand— in the plant that will serve as food for the caterpillars. They can lay them either in clusters of different shapes or singly. There are even females that release their eggs while they are flying over a meadow.

In some species the shape, color, and size of males and females may differ. The males are often smaller.

Right: Different stages of reproduction: ① Courtship occurs during the nuptial flight. The ceremony is usually complicated. Most species perform special courtship flights and "dances." ② Actual mating usually takes place on a plant. ③ Egg-laying.

Below:
A. Courtship between the male and the female.
B. Several ways of laying eggs.

CATERPILLARS CHANGE SKIN

During their lifetime, lepidoptera go through four very different stages: **egg**, **caterpillar**, **pupa** or **chrysalis**, and **adult**.

During this cycle, that can last from some weeks to several years, their bodies undergo great changes. This is called **metamorphosis**.

Out of the egg, which is very different depending on the species, comes the **larva** or caterpillar. The first thing it does is to eat its empty egg. The caterpillar needs a lot of food to accumulate reserves for the following stages.

The caterpillar does not resemble the adult. It has large jaws and glands that produce silk. In addition to six true legs, most caterpillars also have five pairs of false legs. These resemble suction cups that help the caterpillar fasten onto a plant. Some caterpillars have only two pairs of false legs and move in a peculiar way, arching their bodies. These are called **inch worms**.

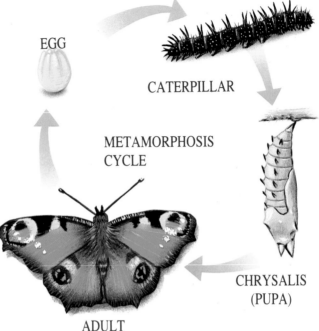

EGG

CATERPILLAR

METAMORPHOSIS CYCLE

CHRYSALIS (PUPA)

ADULT

During its development, the caterpillar sheds or **molts** its skin four or five times. Before each molt, it stops eating. Soon it sheds the old skin and emerges with a new, roomier one. When the development is complete, some caterpillars look for a leaf or twig from which they hang. There they spin a protective silk case called a **cocoon**. Other caterpillars bury themselves in the soil. Both kinds form a chrysalis in which final development takes place.

Right: ① Caterpillars need a lot of food to grow. ② During their development, they will molt four times. ③ An inchworm, which moves by arching its body.

Left: Stages of the metamorphosis.

Below: A caterpillar is very different from the butterfly or moth it will become.

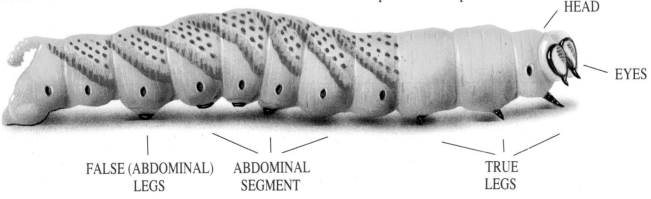

HEAD

EYES

FALSE (ABDOMINAL) LEGS

ABDOMINAL SEGMENT

TRUE LEGS

THE BIRTH OF A BUTTERFLY OR MOTH

After the last molt the caterpillar becomes a chrysalis. During this stage it does not move or eat. But important changes are taking place inside.

The chrysalis of most butterflies hang upside down from a leaf or branch, fastened by means of thin threads of silk woven by the caterpillar. However, many moths construct a cocoon of twigs or mud.

Some of them even remain underground until they emerge as adults.

When the adult is completely formed, it breaks the skin of the chrysalis and chews through the cocoon. Immediately after emerging, it expels the liquid accumulated during the chrysalis stage. In some species, it is red in color. Since it is not unusual for all butterflies to emerge at the same time in the same area, the ground often becomes red.

In the beginning, the butterflies' wings are soft and folded, and the butterfly cannot fly. It hangs from a branch, holding on with its legs, and stretches its wings little by little. The butterfly remains in the sun for some hours drying its wings. At last it is able to fly.

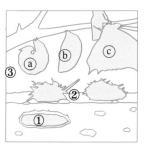

Right: The different kinds of chrysalis. ① A chrysalis buried underground. ② A chrysalis protected by a cocoon made of mud and twigs. ③ Chrysalises hanging from a branch show ⓐ developing and ⓑ full-grown pupa; ⓒ the adult form leaving the cocoon.

Left: Process of metamorphosis:
Butterfly: (1) The caterpillar forms a chrysalis. (2) The chrysalis hangs from a branch. (3) Birth of the adult. (4) The adult stretches its wings.
Moth: (1) The caterpillar starts weaving its cocoon. (2) The chrysalis forms inside the cocoon. (3) The adult emerges. (4) The adult stretches its wings.

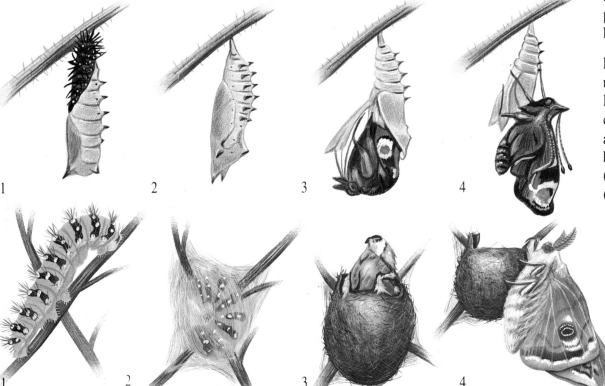

1 2 3 4

1 2 3 4

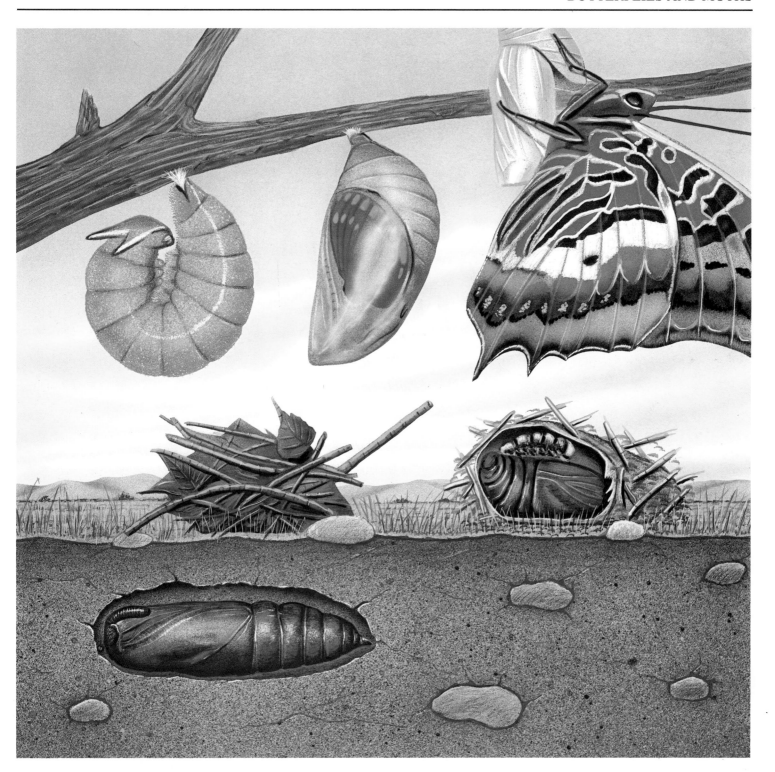

HOW DO THEY FEED?

Butterflies and moths feed during the caterpillar stage, and many of them also feed when they are adult.

The caterpillars mainly eats plants. Depending on the species, they prefer different parts of the plant: leaves, buds, flowers, seeds, or roots.

Some of them eat the inside parts of a plant or fruit, live inside, and dig long tunnels. There are also a large number of moths or caterpillars that feed on feathers, leather, cloth, carpets, cardboard, flour. Some of them even eat other insects.

The adult's nourishment is very different. With their spiral tube, most of them sip the nectar of flowers and the sweet juices of ripe fruit.

Some lepidoptera do not feed when they are adult and live on the reserves accumulated when they were caterpillars. These species do not have a spiral tube.

There is a small group of butterflies that have jaws like caterpillars instead of tubes; they chew the pollen of flowers.

Butterflies and moths also need water that they obtain from dew, from wet ground, or directly from ponds.

Above: Leaf-miner caterpillars create furrows on leaves that resemble extra-ordinary mazes.

TRACK LEFT BY THE CATERPILLARS

Right: Larvae and adults feed in different ways. ① Many butterflies sip the flowers' nectar with their proboscis. ② Caterpillars feed on different parts of the plant. ③ Some caterpillars tunnel great distances to find their food.

ADULTS CHEWING POLLEN

Right: These butterflies have no spiral proboscis but they have strong jaws with which to chew pollen grains.

MANY ENEMIES

Butterflies and moths have many enemies at all stages—when they are eggs, larvae, in the chrysalis stage, or as adults. All the animals that feed on insects are their enemies: frogs and reptiles such as the chameleon capture them with their sticky tongues. Many birds and mammals also prefer moths and butterflies.

The main enemy of the night-flying moths is the bat. These flying mammals emit ultrasounds to help them locate the moths in flight.

The day-flying butterflies are also in danger. Spiders prepare invisible webs to capture them. Other insects can capture them too, such as praying mantises and certain beetles.

Solitary wasps paralyze caterpillars with their long sting and take them to their nest to feed their larvae.

If butterflies had no natural enemies, their numbers would be very large, since each female lays a great number of eggs. This would be harmful not only for plants, but also for the butterflies themselves, because food would become scarce.

Right: Lepidoptera have many different enemies during all stages of their development. Here we see beetles that eat caterpillars ①, frogs ②, and chameleons ③ that capture butterflies with their sticky tongues, birds that feed on insects ④, etc.
Left: This solitary wasp has paralyzed a caterpillar. Now it places it in its nest to feed its larvae.

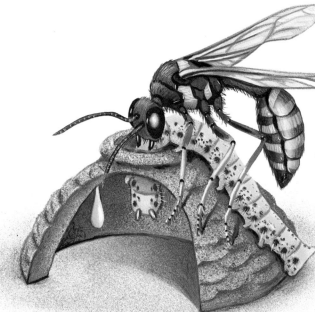

Right: Bats are moths' most dangerous enemies. Their extraordinary "radar" locates insects while they are flying.

GUESS WHERE THEY ARE

Butterflies and moths protect themselves from their numerous enemies by using different defense strategies, depending on which stage they are in.

Females lay eggs among plants to hide them; some species even cover them with fibers. Caterpillars hide themselves in a plant or underground.

However, much more efficient is **camouflage**. This ingenious system of blending with the habitat, is used by many lepidoptera—as adults, caterpillars, and chrysalises.

There are species of moths that imitate the color and shape of things around them, such as leaves, stones, or tree bark.

Certain caterpillars become almost invisible when they stay motionless on a branch.

Many butterflies have bright, showy colors to attract a partner. But the reverse side of their wings has a confusing pattern that actually conceals them. When they are not flying, they fold their wings vertically and become almost invisible.

CHANGING COLOR TO ADAPT TO THE ENVIRONMENT

Right: ① Eggs hidden by fibers. ② Chrysalis that resembles a leaf. ③ Caterpillars that resemble a twig. ④ Adult that blends with the trunk it is on. ⑤ Adult with folded wings can barely be seen among the leaves. ⑥ The same adult with wings spread out.

CAMOUFLAGE COLORS

FIRST PAIR OF WINGS, UNFOLDED

Above: This moth species evolves different coloration in response to the sootiness of the industrial area where it lives. Lighter moths are easily seen by birds and eaten; darker moths escape predators.

Left: Butterfly hiding its bright colors; below, showing the startling "eyes" of its second pair of wings.

BRILLIANT BUTTERFLIES

Many caterpillars, chrysalises, and adults do not need to hide because they are poisonous or produce substances with unpleasant tastes.

Certain caterpillars have bodies covered with spines or with hairs that cause itching and drives their enemies away.

The caterpillar of the cabbage butterfly gives off a repelling substance that is green in color, and the monarch butterfly, when annoyed, emits a bad-smelling liquid.

Species that are poisonous have brilliant colors that warn potential predators of their deadly poison.

NONPOISONOUS
BUTTERFLY

POISONOUS
BUTTERFLY

Right: In this illustration you can see various cases of mimicry. These butterflies, which have no scales on their wings, are mistaken for wasps or bees. This usually frightens off predators.

Left, above: This is an example of mimicry. These two butterflies look as if they are of the same species, but it is a trick of nature. Only the bottom one is a poisonous butterfly.

Left: Poisonous caterpillar in a defensive position. Its bright colors are not for show but are a warning to its enemies: "If you eat me, I won't be good for you."

All butterflies of the same species have the same designs and colors. This makes it easy for other insects and animals to recognize and stay away from the ones that are harmful.

There are also harmless butterflies that copy the designs and colors of the poisonous species. They are called **mimetic** butterflies. Sometimes they resemble each other so much that it is very difficult to tell them apart. These butterflies outwit their enemies by posing as dangerous so that their enemies are afraid to approach them. Some mimetic butterflies resemble other insects, such as bees or wasps. Their wings are transparent and they have black and yellow stripes on their abdomen.

THEY GO AWAY...BUT WILL THEY COME BACK?

Just like many birds, some butterfly species migrate hundreds or thousands of miles during certain periods of the year.

These butterflies are good fliers and most of them travel in groups that may number in the thousands.

In most migrating species the butterflies that go away are not the same ones that come back. In Europe and Africa, butterflies fly to the north in the spring to reproduce and then they die. Their descendants come back to the region of origin in the winter.

The monarch butterfly that lives in the United States is one of the few species that leaves and then returns. Its migrations are very impressive. In the fall, it flies south in groups to California and Mexico. Some monarch butterflies even cross the Atlantic Ocean to the Canary Islands and Europe.

Monarch butterflies migrate in search of warmer weather to spend the winter, and thousands of them gather together. When mild weather arrives, they come back north. But not all of them succeed.

Right: Monarch butterflies gathering together for the migration of more than 2,000 miles (more than 3,000 km) that will lead them to California and Mexico. When the winter is over, they will return home.

Right: Map with the routes of different migrating butterflies. Note the long distances they can travel while looking for the warm weather they need to live and reproduce.

DANAUS PLEXIPUS

CYNTHIA CARDUI

AUTOGRAPHA GAMMA

HERSE CONVOLVULI

LONG PROCESSIONS

ADULT OF
THE PINE
PROCESSIONAL

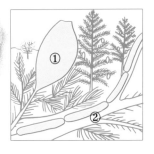

Some caterpillars display odd behavior: They are sociable—like bees. After they hatch, they gather and live together inside a nest of silk that they themselves make.

The caterpillars of the pine processional species build large nests in pine trees. If you find one, do not touch it! This caterpillar has hairs that cause itching.

Few animals dare approach them, but some birds and the small red ant do not mind attacking them.

These caterpillars remain in the shelter during the day and go out at night to look for food. They always walk in procession, following the silk thread that the leader spins from glands in its head.

When they find food, they separate. Then, when they have eaten enough, they gather again and follow the silk thread to return to the nest.

The caterpillar can cause great damage to pine forests because it strips the branches of pine needles.

Above: Example of a pine processional adult. During this stage they are harmless to conifer forests.

Below: Red ants are the pine processional caterpillars worst enemy. The caterpillar's irritating hairs cannot stop the attack of these little insects.

Right: Pine processional caterpillars build large nests ①, which they leave in long processions ② in their search for food. They separate for eating, during which time they can cause great damage to the trees they live in.

RED ANTS
ATTACKING A
PINE PROCESSIONAL
CATERPILLAR

THE SILKWORM

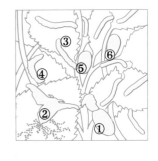

The **silk industry** started in China about 3,000 years ago. Today the silk industry is still very important, not only in Asian countries, such as China, India, and Japan, but in European countries as well.

Silk is made by the caterpillars of certain moths. The most valued is the silk produced by the "silkworm."

When the weather is good, the female silk moth lays a great number of eggs. After the winter, the caterpillars hatch. They only eat the leaves of the mulberry tree.

The caterpillars grow quickly, molting their skin four times in one month. Before becoming chrysalises, they produce a long silk thread with which they weave a cocoon. This single thread can be more than half mile (1 km) in length and is wound around and around the caterpillar that makes it.

In order to obtain silk, the cocoons are harvested before the chrysalises change into adult moths, which would destroy the cocoons as they emerged.

Then the process of metamorphosis is halted, as the cocoon is softened by dipping in hot water. Afterwards, the silk of the cocoon is unwound to get the thread with which delicate cloth will be made.

Right: Different stages in the metamorphosis of the silkworm: ① Adult form leaving the cocoon. ② Female laying eggs; 300 to 700 eggs are typical. ③ Caterpillars eating the leaves of the mulberry tree. ④ Caterpillar spinning its cocoon. ⑤ and ⑥ Different stages of the development of the cocoon.

ADULT SILK MOTH

CATERPILLARS ("SILKWORMS")

EGGS

COCOONS

Above, right and below: Illustration of the process of producing silk, as it has been done since time immemorial.

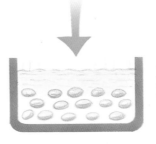

DIPPING COCOONS IN HOT WATER

FABRIC

PROCESS OF SPINNING SILK

SERIOUS DAMAGE

Below: Butterflies in their adult stage help in pollination. When they land on a flower the pollen grains stick to their legs. This pollen falls on another flower, fertilizing it.

Right: Caterpillars can become dangerous pests. These caterpillars, before becoming cabbage butterflies, have damaged a cabbage farm.

Caterpillars eat constantly and may cause serious damage both to agriculture (they attack crops, fruit trees, orchards, and so on), and to forests.

The hairy caterpillar of the oak tree and the processional caterpillar damage large sections of forests by weakening trees. Some moths damage stored grain, corn, flour, clothes, paper, etc.

Sometimes humans are the cause of this destruction—for instance, when the caterpillars' enemies are eliminated with insecticide, they no longer eat caterpillars.

Although many caterpillars are harmful to humans, adult butterflies are inoffensive. On the contrary, they are very useful because they pollinate plants by carrying pollen from flower to flower.

However, humans can damage many species of butterflies by destroying their habitats and hunting them for collections. Because of this, many species are in danger and must be protected.

Right: A caterpillar digging tunnels inside an apple that it is feeding on.

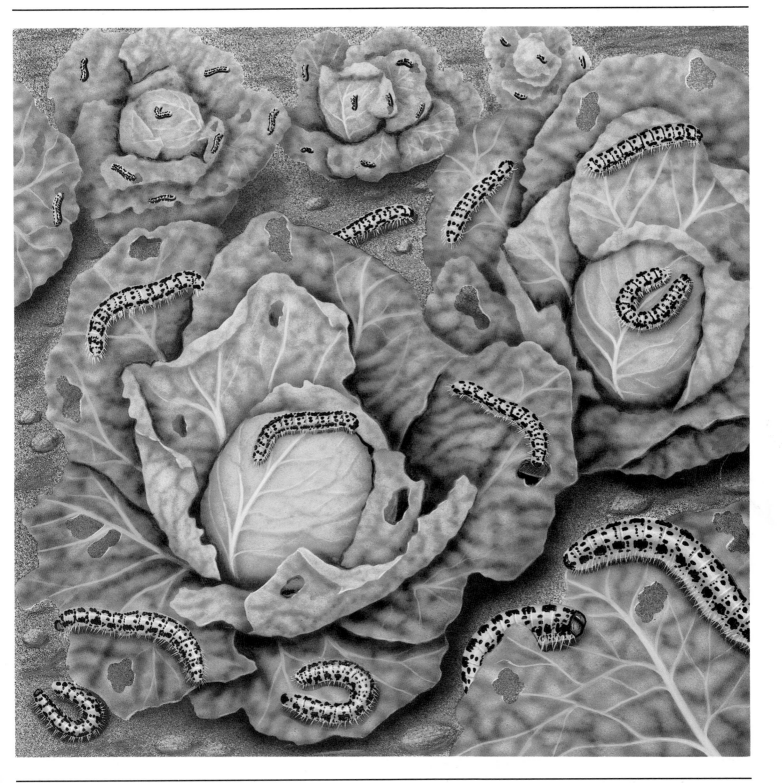

Glossary

abdomen. The back part of the body behind the thorax.

antenna. Organ of sensation located on the head of the moth or butterfly.

camouflage. Coloration, and sometimes shape, of an animal that visually blends into the creature's surroundings making its detection difficult.

caterpillar. Wormlike larva of the butterfly.

chrysalis. Stage in the development of a butterfly, between the caterpillar and adult states; also called a pupa.

cocoon. Silk case that protects the chrysalises of certain butterflies and moths.

facets. Tiny units that make up the compound eye of the butterfly and moth.

inch worm. Type of caterpillar with only two pairs of false legs; it moves by arching its body.

larva. Phase in the development of insects; the larva of moths and butterflies are caterpillars.

Lepidoptera. An order of insects that have wings covered with scales; it includes butterflies and moths.

metamorphosis. Complete transformation that occurs in the body of some insects, such as butterflies and moths, during their development.

migration. Periodic or occasional movement animals undertake from one place to another, owing to reasons of climate, reproduction, or availability of food.

mimesis. Mimicry of color, form, and sometimes even behavior of another species.

nectar. Sweet liquid that many flowers produce.

nuptial flight. Flight that many butterflies and moths undertake prior to mating for the purpose of finding a partner.

pheromones. Substances secreted by certain female lepidoptera to attract a mating partner.

pollination. Conveying pollen from the stamen of one flower to the female parts of another, thus achieving reproduction of the plant.

proboscis. The long, flexible tube that certain lepidoptera use to sip nectar from flowers.

pupa. See chrysalis.

thorax. The center part of the body of a moth or butterfly to which six thin legs and two large pairs of wings are attached.

Index

Boldface numbers indicate illustrations